IF..

a Poem by Rudyard Kipling

Eric Johnson

IF.. a Poem by Rudyard Kipling

Republished: 2023
Original Text: 1888
Enhanced with Illustrations: 2023

Copyright 2023 by Eric Johnson

This edition of "**IF.. a Poem by Rudyard Kipling**" is a reproduction of the original text, which is in the public domain. The enhancements, including illustrations and any other additional content, have been created specifically for this edition and are protected by copyright.

All rights reserved. No part of this publication may be reproduced, distributed, or transmitted in any form or by any means, including photocopying, recording, or other electronic or mechanical methods, without the prior written permission of the publisher, except in the case of brief quotations embodied in critical reviews and certain other noncommercial uses permitted by copyright law.

The public domain status of the original text is not affected by this publication. The enhancements, including illustrations and any additional content, are protected by copyright 2023 by Eric Johnson.

ISBN: 9798868208751

This book is dedicated to:

INTRODUCTION:

IN THE FOLLOWING PAGES, EMBARK ON A VISUAL JOURNEY THROUGH THE TIMELESS WISDOM OF RUDYARD KIPLING'S "IF." EACH PASSAGE OF THIS CLASSIC POEM IS ACCOMPANIED BY AN ILLUSTRATION CAREFULLY CRAFTED TO ILLUMINATE THE PROFOUND LESSONS IT IMPARTS. AS YOU TURN THE PAGES, LET THE FUSION OF WORDS AND IMAGES GUIDE YOU THROUGH A TAPESTRY OF VIRTUES, RESILIENCE, AND THE INDOMITABLE SPIRIT OF HUMAN CHARACTER. "IF" INVITES REFLECTION, AND THESE ILLUSTRATIONS SERVE AS VISUAL COMPANIONS, ENRICHING THE EXPERIENCE OF KIPLING'S POETIC MASTERPIECE.

IF

RUDYARD KIPLING

IF YOU CAN KEEP YOUR HEAD WHEN
ALL ABOUT YOU ARE LOSING THEIRS
AND BLAMING IT ON YOU,

IF YOU CAN TRUST YOURSELF WHEN ALL MEN DOUBT YOU, BUT MAKE ALLOWANCE FOR THEIR DOUBTING TOO;

IF YOU CAN WAIT AND NOT BE TIRED BY WAITING, OR BEING LIED ABOUT, DON'T DEAL IN LIES,

OR BEING HATED, DON'T GIVE WAY TO HATING, AND YET DON'T LOOK TOO GOOD, NOR TALK TOO WISE;

IF YOU CAN DREAM—AND NOT MAKE DREAMS YOUR MASTER;
IF YOU CAN THINK—AND NOT MAKE THOUGHTS YOUR AIM;

IF YOU CAN MEET WITH TRIUMPH AND DISASTER AND TREAT THOSE TWO IMPOSTORS JUST THE SAME;

IF YOU CAN BEAR TO HEAR THE TRUTH
YOU'VE SPOKEN TWISTED BY KNAVES TO
MAKE A TRAP FOR FOOLS,

OR WATCH THE THINGS YOU GAVE YOUR
LIFE TO, BROKEN, AND STOOP AND
BUILD 'EM UP WITH WORN-OUT TOOLS:

IF YOU CAN MAKE ONE HEAP OF ALL
YOUR WINNINGS AND RISK IT ON ONE
TURN OF PITCH-AND-TOSS,

AND LOSE, AND START AGAIN AT YOUR
BEGINNINGS AND NEVER BREATHE A
WORD ABOUT YOUR LOSS;

IF YOU CAN FORCE YOUR HEART AND
NERVE AND SINEW
TO SERVE YOUR TURN LONG AFTER THEY
ARE GONE,

AND SO HOLD ON WHEN THERE IS NOTHING IN YOU EXCEPT THE WILL WHICH SAYS TO THEM: 'HOLD ON!'

IF YOU CAN TALK WITH CROWDS AND KEEP YOUR VIRTUE,
OR WALK WITH KINGS—NOR LOSE THE COMMON TOUCH,

IF NEITHER FOES NOR LOVING FRIENDS
CAN HURT YOU,
IF ALL MEN COUNT WITH YOU, BUT NONE
TOO MUCH;

IF.. A Poem by Rudyard Kipling

IF YOU CAN FILL THE UNFORGIVING MINUTE WITH SIXTY SECONDS' WORTH OF DISTANCE RUN,

YOURS IS THE EARTH AND EVERYTHING THAT'S IN IT,
AND—WHICH IS MORE—YOU'LL BE A MAN, MY SON!

IF

RUDYARD KIPLING

IF YOU CAN KEEP YOUR HEAD WHEN ALL ABOUT YOU
ARE LOSING THEIRS AND BLAMING IT ON YOU,

IF YOU CAN TRUST YOURSELF WHEN ALL MEN DOUBT
YOU, BUT MAKE ALLOWANCE FOR THEIR DOUBTING
TOO;

IF YOU CAN WAIT AND NOT BE TIRED BY WAITING, OR
BEING LIED ABOUT, DON'T DEAL IN LIES,

OR BEING HATED, DON'T GIVE WAY TO HATING, AND
YET DON'T LOOK TOO GOOD, NOR TALK TOO WISE;

IF YOU CAN DREAM—AND NOT MAKE DREAMS YOUR
MASTER;
    IF YOU CAN THINK—AND NOT MAKE THOUGHTS
YOUR AIM;

IF YOU CAN MEET WITH TRIUMPH AND DISASTER
    AND TREAT THOSE TWO IMPOSTORS JUST THE SAME;

IF YOU CAN BEAR TO HEAR THE TRUTH YOU'VE SPOKEN
    TWISTED BY KNAVES TO MAKE A TRAP FOR FOOLS,

OR WATCH THE THINGS YOU GAVE YOUR LIFE TO,
BROKEN,

    AND STOOP AND BUILD 'EM UP WITH WORN-OUT TOOLS;

IF YOU CAN MAKE ONE HEAP OF ALL YOUR WINNINGS
    AND RISK IT ON ONE TURN OF PITCH-AND-TOSS,

AND LOSE, AND START AGAIN AT YOUR BEGINNINGS
    AND NEVER BREATHE A WORD ABOUT YOUR LOSS;

IF YOU CAN FORCE YOUR HEART AND NERVE AND SINEW
    TO SERVE YOUR TURN LONG AFTER THEY ARE GONE,

AND SO HOLD ON WHEN THERE IS NOTHING IN YOU
    EXCEPT THE WILL WHICH SAYS TO THEM: 'HOLD ON!'

IF YOU CAN TALK WITH CROWDS AND KEEP YOUR VIRTUE,
    OR WALK WITH KINGS—NOR LOSE THE COMMON TOUCH,

IF NEITHER FOES NOR LOVING FRIENDS CAN HURT YOU,
    IF ALL MEN COUNT WITH YOU, BUT NONE TOO MUCH;

IF YOU CAN FILL THE UNFORGIVING MINUTE
    WITH SIXTY SECONDS' WORTH OF DISTANCE RUN,

YOURS IS THE EARTH AND EVERYTHING THAT'S IN IT,
    AND—WHICH IS MORE—YOU'LL BE A MAN, MY SON!

IF.. A Poem by Rudyard Kipling

Joseph Rudyard Kipling (1865 - 1936) was an English novelist, short-story writer, poet, and journalist. He was born in British India, which inspired much of his work.

Printed in Great Britain
by Amazon